Be a DINOSAUR DETECTIVE

Purnell

Be a DINOSAUR DETECTIVE

Written by
DOUGAL DIXON MSc

Illustrated by
STEVE LINGS

First published in Great Britain in 1987
by Macdonald & Co (Publishers) Ltd,
London & Sydney
A BPCC plc company

Devised and produced by Templar Publishing Ltd,
107 High Street, Dorking, Surrey RH4 1QA

Copyright © 1987 by Templar Publishing Ltd
Illustrations copyright © 1987 by Templar Publishing Ltd

Edited by Nicholas Bellenberg
Designed by Peter Marriage
Colour separations by Positive Colour Ltd, Maldon, Essex
Printed in Great Britain by Purnell (Book Production) Ltd,
Member of the BPCC Group

Macdonald and Co (Publishers) Ltd,
Greater London House, Hampstead Road, London NW1 7QX

British Library Cataloguing in Publication Data
Dixon, Dougal
Be a dinosaur detective
1. Dinosaurs – Juvenile literature
I. Title
567.9'1   QE862.D5

ISBN 0-361-07795-5

C O N T E N T S

Fossil follies

Pretend you lived over 200 years ago. You would never have heard of fossils, as no-one knew what they were. Imagine you were walking along a beach, where the cliffs were being worn away by the sea – or scrambling in a mountain gully where a waterfall tumbled down a hillside – and you found one of these strange things.

This is a fossil, today called an ammonite. What would you think it was just by looking at it?

The best guess that people 200 years ago could come up with, was that these were the remains of long-dead snakes.

This peculiar looking thing is a skull. No-one was in any doubt about that.

But the "experts" from 200 years ago guessed wrongly about the skull's owner. They thought it belonged to a giant Cyclops (a one-eyed man in ancient stories).

In fact

Today we know that ammonites are the coiled shells of octopus-like animals.

In fact

Nowadays it is taken for granted that the skull belonged to a type of elephant called a mammoth. The big hole in the middle of the "forehead" is not an eye hole, but the nostril where the trunk was attached.

These bullet-like objects are made of rock. Could you work out what they used to be?

One common idea 200 years ago was that these mysterious things were in fact thunderbolts.

This rock covered in fossil sea shells was found by a waterfall up a mountain. It was nowhere near the sea.

As they were found so far away from the sea, people thought that the shells were left up the mountain by the great Flood mentioned in the Bible. In this, everyone – apart from Noah and his animals – died.

In fact

The "thunderbolts" were actually the fossilised shells of squid-like animals. These fossils are called belemnites.

In fact

The shell-covered rock was found high above the sea, because the mountains themselves were formed from rocks that once made up the sea bed. They have been forced into new forms by the natural actions of the Earth's crust.

False starts

200 years ago people didn't know much about the world around them. Nowadays there is a solid background of science which we use to help us come up with new theories. Most of today's scientists' ideas come from fossils – like those shown on these two pages. Fossils are the remains of dead animals and plants preserved in rock for millions of years.

When people started to take fossils seriously, they encountered a few problems. In 1725 these fake fossils were made out of clay by some university professors and students who wanted to fool another professor. The poor man was confused for years!

This skeleton of a "sea-serpent" was put together by a hoaxer in 1846. He made it out of the fossil bones of some whales. Many great scientists were fooled by it.

The world of the past

How do we know what the world was like a very long time ago? Well, we can look at the rocks. There are three different types of rocks. One type is formed when hot molten stuff (lava) from inside the Earth cools and becomes hard. Another forms when an already existing rock is squeezed or "cooked" inside the Earth and turns into something new. The third type forms from sand and mud and gravel, which piles up on a sea bed or river bed. Let's look at this third type here. It is called "sedimentary rock".

Make some sedimentary rock

2. Now pour in a layer of mud mixed with plaster-of-Paris. Add a layer of gravel and another layer of sand. These layers should be mixed with dry plaster-of-Paris too.

1. Take a plastic sweet jar and pour a few centimetres of dry sand mixed with the same amount of plaster-of-Paris into it.

In the real world, the first layer of sand may have formed on a river bed.

Then the river may have been flooded by the sea. The mud layer would then have formed on top of the sand at the bottom of the sea.

Next, the sea may have dried up and a shingle beach may have formed to make yet another new layer.

Rock formation
Here are some pictures of rocks that show how they were formed.

This rock formed from clay in a pond. The pond dried up and the clay cracked in the hot sun. You can now see the shapes of these cracks in the rock.

These great curved beds are actually fossil sand dunes. This shows that the sandstone in this cliff was once a desert.

Where do you think this one formed?

3. Look at how the mass has formed different layers. While you are pouring these layers, drop in a few seashells as well. Then add water, until all the layers are saturated. Leave it to set for a couple of days.

4. When it all hardens, split the plastic jar open. The different layers should look something like the rock of a cliff face. You should be able to split this open, along the different layers. Then you will find your seashells again.

Finally, a desert may have spread gradually to cover the whole area. Millions of years later, water may have seeped through all these layers, and left minerals stuck between the grains – just like your plaster-of-Paris did. These minerals would have cemented the grains into rock.

Any animals that lived in the river, the sea, the shore or the desert, would have left their bones and shells in this rock. Over millions of years these would have been turned into fossils.

CLIFF CLUES

Here is a cliff made from the rocks that were laid down by the real-life ancient river, sea, shore and desert. We have left holes for the fossils. **Where do you think you would find the oldest rock? At the top or the bottom?**

DESERT

SHORE

SEA BED

RIVER BED

Here are the kinds of fossils that we would expect to find in the different layers, or beds, of rocks. **See if you can match them to their rock types.**

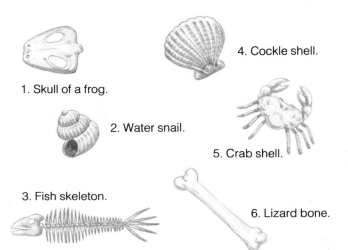

1. Skull of a frog.

2. Water snail.

3. Fish skeleton.

4. Cockle shell.

5. Crab shell.

6. Lizard bone.

Animals through the ages

The Earth is old, older than you can possibly imagine. In fact, it is about 4,500,000,000 (four thousand, five hundred million) years old. Life probably started on the Earth about 3,500,000,000 (three thousand, five hundred million) years ago. The first living things were only tiny soft blobs. It was not until about 570,000,000 (five hundred and seventy million) years ago that animals with hard shells and skeletons appeared. This is how old the oldest identifiable fossils are.

All these figures are a bit much to take in. So geologists have split up the Earth's history into chunks called **eras** and **periods** and have given them different names – just as we split up a year into months with different names. The whole thing together is called the **geological column**. All the different changes that take place – like new plants and animals appearing – are together called **evolution**.

ERA		AGE (Million years)	PERIOD	LIFE FORMS
CAINOZOIC	Quaternary	TODAY — 0	Recent	The Ice Age. Woolly mammals lived through the cold. Now the last animal to appear suddenly became important – the human! Eventually modern human beings evolved.
		0.01	Pleistocene	
		2	Pliocene	
	Tertiary	7	Miocene	Now that the big reptiles were gone – and we still don't know why – the mammals became the most important animals and evolved quickly. Early apes appeared.
		26	Oligocene	
		38	Eocene	
		54	Palaeocene	
		65		
MESOZOIC			Cretaceous	The dinosaurs and the other big reptiles flourished until the end of this period. Then they all mysteriously died out.
		136	Jurassic	More forests and swamps spread over the land. The dinosaurs grew to be mighty beasts. The first bird evolved.
		195	Triassic	There were still many deserts. The reptiles began to branch out and change into mammals. The first dinosaurs appeared.
		225	Permian	Deserts began to take the place of the forests. Reptiles, like big lizards and crocodiles, began to take the place of the amphibians.
PALAEOZOIC		280	Carboniferous	Great forests covered the lowlands. Huge creatures that could live on land or in water (called amphibians), lived there.
		345	Devonian	Rivers and lakes were full of fishes. The first animals were leaving the water – including some fish that could actually breathe air.
		395	Silurian	The first plants were moving out of the water to take their places on the land. Giant sea scorpions were common in the water.
		440	Ordovician	There was still only sea life, but fish were beginning to evolve. There were many trilobites and other hard-bodied animals.
		500	Cambrian	The only life at this time was in the sea. Crab-like and shrimp-like animals lived there and these gave us the first fossils.
		570	Precambrian	
		4500	Origin of Earth	

Invertebrates

Fish

Amphibians

Early Reptiles

Mammals

Sea reptiles

Lizards & snakes

Crocodiles

Pterosaurs

Dinosaurs

Birds

Dinosaurs

The word "dinosaur" means "terrible lizard". It is a name for the main group of extinct reptiles of the Mesozoic era. Dinosaurs, like fish, amphibia, mammals and the other reptiles, all have backbones. Animals with backbones are called vertebrates.

The dinosaurs lived in the Triassic, Jurassic and Cretaceous periods – between 230 and 65 million years ago. These three periods are together called the Mesozoic era. We shall be interested in this era for the rest of this book.

The big skeleton

A scientist interested in dinosaurs would be very lucky to find a complete dinosaur skeleton. Usually dinosaur remains are just made up of scattered bones. And even if the skeleton is complete, the bones will usually be all jumbled up. You can see the mixed-up remains of one complete dinosaur skeleton on this page. You will see that these remains also include the skull. The skull is usually missing from real skeletons. That is because dinosaurs'

skulls were so lightly built that they often broke before they could become fossils.

Trace over the shapes of the pieces. Then draw them on thick paper or thin card and piece the bits together to make a whole dinosaur. Once you have assembled your skeleton, jumble it all up again. Then throw half the pieces away, and try to build it again. This is more like the problem given to scientists by real skeletons that they dig out of the rocks.

A fossil poser

Which of the dinosaurs shown here are most likely to become fossilized? **Can you guess why?**

Skeleton skills

Here are some jumbled-up dinosaur skeletons, just as they were found in the rocks. **See if you can identify them from the pictures in the rest of the book.**

This one was found in the late Jurassic rocks in North America. Look at the broad plates lying near the backbone as a clue to its name.

This is a very good skeleton, as fossil skeletons go, even though only half of it remains. It is from the late Cretaceous and was found in North America. Notice the great curving crest on the skull.

Dancing dinosaurs?

Sometimes dinosaur remains consist only of footprints. Here is a trail of fossil footprints belonging to two dinosaurs. **Can you tell what happened?**

⋆⋆ **ANSWERS** ⋆⋆

A FOSSIL POSER
The dinosaurs in or near the water would be the most likely to become fossils if they died. This is because their bodies would be covered in mud which would harden and, in time, preserve the bones as stone.

SKELETON SKILLS
The Jurassic skeleton belonged to a *Stegosaurus*. The late Cretaceous skeleton used to be a *Parasaurolophus*.

DANCING DINOSAURS?
One theory about these footprints says that the owner of the small feet was caught by the large-footed dinosaur, and turned into a meal. Of course, you might have other ideas.

13

Meat-eating dinosaurs

Everything that we know about dinosaurs – and all other prehistoric animals – is deduced from the evidence and clues found in their fossils.

The different shapes of dinosaur bodies, and the bones that they are made from, tell us a lot about their way of life.

Here, and over the page, you can find out all about what meat-eating dinosaurs were like and how they used to live.

TEETH

The teeth of a meat-eating dinosaur were sharp, and often had edges like those on a saw, as they had to cut through meat. This is a tooth from the largest meat-eater – Tyrannosaurus.

SKULL

A dinosaur's skull was full of holes. This kept it light. A meat-eater's skull was made from many pieces, loosely held together. This meant that it could change shape slightly to let the animal swallow large chunks of meat. **Which of the dinosaurs shown over the page owned this horned skull?**

ARMS

The arms, called forelimbs, were usually used to hold prey.

This tiny limb has only two fingers. It belonged to the biggest meat-eater of them all. Its arms could only have been used to push the dinosaur off the ground when it was getting to its feet. **Look at the next spread to find out who the dinosaur was.**

This enormous arm is from a meat-eating dinosaur called *Deinocheirus*. It is 2.6 metres long. We don't know anything about the rest of its body.

Make a meat-eating dinosaur

Get some modelling clay about the size of a tennis ball, one long pencil and two short ones, a spring clothes-peg and two spent matchsticks.

1. Take a large lump of modelling clay and mould it into a ball. Now stick the two short pencils into it. These are the dinosaur's legs. Put a small clay "foot" on the end of each pencil.

2. The teeth and jaws are very important. The dinosaur used these to kill its food. The clothes-peg makes the dinosaur's jaws.

3. Your dinosaur's jaws make it very heavy at the front. You'll probably find that it falls over. To make it balance, the meat-eater needs a tail at the back.

4. Finally, use the matchsticks to make the dinosaur's forelimbs. Stick them into the front, near the head, where they can reach the jaws.

All the meat-eating dinosaurs were built to this design – but not out of modelling clay! All the different meat-eating dinosaurs shown over the page have this basic shape.

LEGS

The two hind legs of the meat-eating dinosaur carried all its weight.
See if you can match the two straight legs on the right with their owners, shown overleaf.

Here is a foot used for killing. That huge claw on the second toe must have been used to slash the dinosaur's victim to death. The other big toes were used for walking.

This leg is about 4 metres long. Look how thick the bones are. It must have supported an enormous animal. It had three huge toes that touched the ground, and one small one that did not.

This leg is long and slim. We know it must have belonged to a swift-running animal, because it looks like the leg of an ostrich.

★ ANSWERS ★

SKULL
Ceratosaurus owned the horned skull.

ARMS
The little arms belonged to Tyrannosaurus.

LEGS
Dromicelomimus used to run with the slim leg, while Tyrannosaurus stood on the giant one.

Famous meat-eaters

This is how big you would be compared to these dinosaurs. Imagine what it would be like to have lived when they were around!

Tyrannosaurus (tyrant lizard). As far as we know, this was the biggest meat-eater of the lot. It was 12 metres long and lived in North America and China in late Cretaceous times.

Food

See if you can guess which of the meat-eating dinosaurs on these pages ate these different types of meat.

Dead animals Probably eaten by dinosaurs too large and slow to catch live food.

Large live animals Eaten by dinosaurs that had special big claws that could kill them.

Smaller live animals These would have been caught and eaten by the powerful hunters which were between 5 and 10 metres long.

Lizards and insects These must have been eaten by the smallest meat-eaters.

Eggs Meat-eating dinosaurs with no teeth may have eaten other dinosaurs' eggs.

Baryonyx (heavy claw). This recently discovered dinosaur had long crocodile-like jaws with lots of teeth, and a huge claw on each hand. We think it ate fish, hooking them out of the river with its claws – like grizzly bears do today. It was 8 metres long and lived in southern England in early Cretaceous times.

Dromiceiomimus (like an emu). This was a very fleet-footed meat-eater. In fact, it ran faster than a racehorse. It was built like an emu or ostrich, and had no teeth. It was 3.5 metres long and lived in Canada in late Cretaceous times.

Compsognathus (pretty jaw). This was probably the smallest of the meat-eaters – no bigger than a chicken! The birds of today may be descended from a dinosaur like this. It was 60 centimetres long and lived in Germany and France in late Jurassic times.

Deinonychus (terrible claw). Perhaps one of the fiercest hunters that ever lived. Just look at its huge claw! This dinosaur was 4 metres long and lived in North America in early Cretaceous times.

Ceratosaurus (horned lizard). This dinosaur looked like a dragon, with horns on its head and a jagged ridge down its back. It was 6 metres long and lived in North America and East Africa in late Jurassic times.

Long-necked plant-eaters

The dinosaurs were some of the largest animals that ever lived. The largest dinosaurs were all plant-eaters. They had enormously heavy bodies, which were supported on massive legs like tree-trunks, and they all had long necks and tails.

SKULLS

Plant-eating dinosaurs had two main types of skull. The first was long and thin with teeth like a comb. The second was box-like and had teeth like chisels.

Can you match up the shapes of these skulls with the dinosaurs shown overleaf?

(a)

(b)

NECK VERTEBRAE

The bones in the neck — called vertebrae — were very large. They had to be to hold all the muscles that supported the neck. This bone is longer than an arm. It belonged to a very tall dinosaur.

Which one over the page do you think it belonged to?

A HALF-WAY STAGE?

This skeleton belongs to a dinosaur called *Anchisaurus*. It lived in North America in the Triassic period – before the long-necked plant-eaters evolved. Scientists think that it sometimes walked on its hind legs and sometimes on all fours, and many believe that it ate both meat and plants. Animals like this may have been the ancestors of the big plant-eaters.

THE FEET

The feet of a long-necked plant-eater were as big as tea-trays. They had to support an animal weighing as much as a railway engine. They were probably built like elephants' feet, with a thick fibrous cushion beneath the toes to take the weight. There were five toes on each foot. The front foot usually had a big claw, and the back foot had either two or three big claws.

✦ ANSWERS ✦

EGGS
Eggs would have been laid by plant-eating dinosaurs when moving, to stop them piling up and crushing the ones on the bottom.

SKULLS
Skull (a) came from a *Diplodocus*, while skull (b) belonged to a *Camarasaurus*.

NECK VERTEBRAE
It belonged to *Brachiosaurus*.

TAIL VERTEBRAE
It belonged to *Diplodocus*.

Make a big plant-eating dinosaur

1. Start with your model meat-eating dinosaur, that you made on page 15. The plant-eating dinosaurs were evolved from small meat-eating dinosaurs.

3. Your dinosaur will fall over because its tail will not be able to balance it any more. Make the front legs much bigger (using two more half pencils) so that your dinosaur can stand on four feet.

2. Plant-eating animals need much more gut than meat-eating ones. This is because plants need more digestion than meat. Plant-eating dinosaurs therefore need bigger bodies. Make the body of your model longer, by adding more clay.

4. A plant-eating dinosaur will not need great big jaws and huge teeth to kill with. Take the "jaws" away and make a small head from clay. If you stick this straight onto the body the animal will not be able to reach its food. So use some more modelling clay to give it a long-reaching neck.

The big plant-eating dinosaurs were built to this design. All the plant-eating dinosaurs shown overleaf have this basic shape.

We sometimes find polished stones in the stomach area of plant-eaters' skeletons. We think that the dinosaurs swallowed stones to help them grind up food.

EGGS

This is a dinosaur egg. It is as big as a football and was found in France. It seems as if the long-necked plant-eaters laid their eggs in long trails – as if they were laying them while moving along. **Why do you think they would do this?**

TAIL VERTEBRAE

The bones of the tail were also very light and strong. This type had a pair of bony skids below, to protect the flesh of the tail as it dragged along the ground. It belonged to one of the longest dinosaurs. **Look over the page and see which one you think it was.**

Famous long-necked plant-eaters

Most of these animals were absolutely enormous. These tiny figures show the size that you would have been beside them.

Diplodocus (with two beams). Its name comes from the two bony skids that protected the tail as it dragged along the ground. At 27 metres it was one of the longest of the dinosaurs, although quite lightly-built. It lived at the same time and in the same place as *Apatosaurus*.

Mamenchisaurus (lizard from Mamenchi). This was like *Diplodocus*, but it had an extremely long neck – about half the length of the animal. It was about the same length as *Diplodocus* and lived in China in the late Jurassic.

Apatosaurus (headless lizard). This was 20 metres long and lived in North America in the late Jurassic period.

Brachiosaurus (arm lizard). This was one of the tallest of the dinosaurs, reaching up to the height of the top windows of a three-storey house. Its forelimbs were longer than its hind limbs, which is unusual for these dinosaurs. It lived in North America and East Africa in the late Jurassic period.

Bone puzzles

(a)

We don't usually find complete dinosaur skeletons – usually just scattered bones. Here are some incomplete skeletons as they were found. See if you can match them up to the animals on this page.

(b)

ANSWERS

BONE PUZZLES

Remains **(a)** are of an *Opisthocoelicaudia*. Scientists had to guess what its head looked like.

Bones **(b)** used to be a *Mamenchisaurus*.

Camarasaurus
(chambered lizard).
Built like *Brachiosaurus*,
it had a box-like skull
and a short tail. It was
18 metres long and lived
in North America in late
Jurassic times.

Opisthocoelicaudia (tail vertebrae with cups
at the back). Try saying that one a few
times! We don't know what the head and
neck of this dinosaur looked like, but it had a
very strong tail. This, and the muscles of the
hind legs, lead scientists to think that it may
have raised itself on its hind legs to feed off
trees. It was about 12 metres long and lived
in China in the late Cretaceous.

Saltasaurus (lizard from Salta
province). This dinosaur was a bit of
an oddity, since its back was covered
with armour. It was about 12 metres
long and lived in South America in
the late Cretaceous.

21

Two-footed plant-eaters

SKULL SKILLS

Sometimes the dinosaur's "beak" was quite broad and duck-bill-like, and was backed up by huge batteries of grinding teeth. Some dinosaurs evolved these duck-bills to help them gather up and eat big mouthfuls of plants. Some of the duck-billed dinosaurs had strange crests on their heads. Here are two duck-billed dinosaur's skulls. **Can you match them up with the animals shown overleaf?**

(a) (b)

HANDS

Some of the plant-eating dinosaurs had five fingers on each hand, but those known as the duck-bills had only four. *Iguanodon* had five fingers. Its first, the thumb, was a huge spike. **What do you think it was used for?**

The duck-bill's hands may have been paddle-like, with webs of skin between the fingers. **What could this have been used for?**

LIFESTYLES

Hypsilophodon was a small two-footed plant-eater. It was about the size of a tree-kangaroo. This led some palaeontologists (fossil experts) to think that it must have climbed trees. We now know that it could not, as its feet were the wrong shape.

The duck-bills had a family life. We know this because we have found nests, still containing fossil babies. The nests were muddy heaps, like those of flamingos. These dinosaurs must have lived in flocks, too, just like flamingos do today.

✦ ANSWERS ✦

HANDS

Iguanodon's huge spike-like thumbs were probably used to pull food into its mouth. They were probably also useful as weapons. A duck-bill's paddle-like hands would have helped it to swim.

SKULL SKILLS

Skull (a) belonged to *Parasaurolophus*, while skull (b) came from a *Tsintaosaurus*.

FEET

The meat-eating dinosaurs had claws with which to catch and kill their prey. Plant-eaters needed their hooves to help them run away from the meat-eaters.

TEETH

The two-legged plant-eaters had teeth that chopped and ground up their plant food. They also had cheek pouches to hold the food while they were chewing it. The hollows in the side of some skulls show where the cheek pouches were. They also had a beak at the front of their mouth. Sometimes the skull was narrow and the beak was quite pointed, like *Iguanodon's*, shown here.

HIPS

This is a hip bone from a two-legged plant-eater. There would have been a space beneath to hold the big gut needed to digest plant-food.

Make a two-footed plant-eater

Remember the long-necked plant-eaters? We found out from looking at them that a plant-eating animal needs a big gut. The two-legged plant-eaters, however, were designed quite differently. You can see how by making another model. Get a big lump of modelling clay to use as the body, some pencils for the legs and tail, and two spent matches.

1. Stick two pencils into the sides of the modelling clay to make the hind legs. The heavy body should hang between the legs, not in front of them. The two-legged plant-eaters had special hip bones to let their bodies work in this way.

2. Now you can add the matches to make the short forearms, and a small lump of modelling clay for the small head. Finish off the dinosaur with a pencil to make the stiff tail which balanced it all.

FEET

The two-footed plant-eaters' feet were usually three toed. They looked like birds' feet. They also looked a bit like the feet of the meat-eaters, so the footprints of the two types of dinosaur are often confused. However, one type all had blunt hooves on the toes, while the other had sharp claws. **Which dinosaurs do you think had which feet?**

TAIL BONES

The vertebrae of these dinosaurs' tails were firmly lashed together by bony tendons (above). This shows that the tails were held stiff and straight.

Famous two-footed plant-eaters

Many of the two-footed plant-eaters were quite small, but some were very big. They are shown to the same scale on this page. Here you are again, compared with them.

Tsintaosaurus (lizard from Tsintao). This was a duck-billed dinosaur 10 metres long. It had a crest that stuck up and forwards from the top of its head. This dinosaur lived in China in the late Cretaceous.

Shantungosaurus (lizard from Shantung). This was the biggest of the duck-billed dinosaurs, and did not have a crest. It was 12 metres long and lived in China in the late Cretaceous.

Iguanodon (iguana toothed – it had teeth like the modern iguana lizard). The first two-footed plant-eater to be discovered, back in 1822. It was 9 metres long and lived in many places in early Cretaceous times. Remains have been found in southern England, France, Belgium, Romania, western North America, North Africa and Mongolia. It was probably hunted by one of the early meat-eaters.

Food

Here are some typical plants of dinosaur times. Which plants do you think were eaten by which dinosaurs on this page?

Horse-tail Vast reed-beds of these grew by the shallow lakes of southern England and northern Europe in the early Cretaceous. They were probably eaten by animals with long, narrow snouts.

Conifers By the end of the Cretaceous period, modern conifers grew everywhere. The fine needles were probably scraped from the twigs by broad-snouted animals, but they would have needed a lot of chewing.

Cycadeoid This was a very common plant, typical of the plants of southern Africa in the Triassic. Its soft young shoots would not have needed much chewing.

★ **ANSWERS** ★

FOOD

Iguanodon would have eaten horse-tails. Conifers must have made good meals for *Parasaurolophus* and others. Cycadeoids were probably eaten by *Lesothosaurus*.

Lesothosaurus (lizard from Lesotho). One of the earliest of the two-footed plant-eaters. It had no beak or cheek-pouches – these had not evolved yet. It was 1 metre long and lived in Lesotho, southern Africa, in late Triassic times.

Hypsilophodon (high-ridged tooth). This was like a miniature *Iguanodon* and must have been a fast runner. It was 1.5 to 2.5 metres long and lived in southern England, Portugal and North America in the early Cretaceous.

Parasaurolophus (almost *Saurolophus* – a similar dinosaur). A duck-billed dinosaur, 10 metres long with a broad snout and a long curving crest. It lived in Canada in the late Cretaceous.

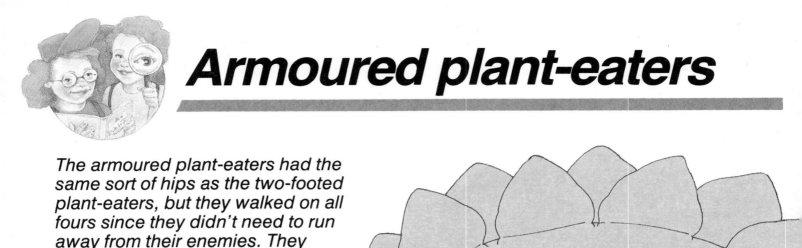

Armoured plant-eaters

The armoured plant-eaters had the same sort of hips as the two-footed plant-eaters, but they walked on all fours since they didn't need to run away from their enemies. They could protect themselves in other ways, as you can see here. Look over the page to find the answers to the questions.

SKULLS

Each type of armoured dinosaur had a different type of skull. You can see a horned dinosaur's skull below. The roofed dinosaurs had small, lightly-built skulls, compared with their bodies. This skull belonged to th biggest roofed dinosaur. **What was its name?**

This bony lump is actually the skull of a welded dinosaur shown overleaf. **Can you guess which one?**

LEGS

Like most of the big plant-eating dinosaurs, the armoured dinosaurs had long hind legs and short front legs. This shows that they evolved from two-footed animals.

.* **ANSWERS** *.

SKULLS
The roofed dinosaur's skull once belonged to a *Stegosaurus*. The welded dinosaur's skull used to be a *Euoplocephalus'* head.

HALF-WAY STAGE
The *Psittacosaurus* could have evolved into a *Protoceratops*.

WEAPONS
The tail spike belonged to *Kentrosaurus*. *Euoplocephalus* had the bony knob at the end of its tail for clubbing attackers. The horned head-shield was used to protect *Triceratops* from its enemies.

WEAPONS

As well as armour to protect themselves, these dinosaurs had weapons so that they could fight back.

The roofed dinosaurs had spikes on their tails, like this. **Look over the page and see if you can guess which roofed dinosaur owned this?**

Which welded dinosaur owned this tail with a bony club at the end?

Which horned dinosaur had these forward-pointing horns on its head shield?

Make an armoured plant-eater

Make the basic shape of a plant-eating animal by following the instructions here. Take a large lump of modelling clay, and stick four half pencils into it for legs. Add a pencil tail at the back and a clay head at the front.

1. A large dinosaur this shape would be too heavy to run away from its enemies. It would have had to defend itself in some way. Cut up some pieces of card to act as armour.

2. The backbone of most animals is the most vulnerable part of their bodies. Stick some armour plates along the backbone to keep away the meat-eaters' great jaws and teeth. All the "roofed dinosaurs" were armoured like this.

3. We can take this type of armour further. Plaster the dinosaur's back with armour plates – like the stones in a pavement. Cover the head with armour too. All the "welded dinosaurs" were armoured like this.

4. A third way of armouring a dinosaur is to stick all the armour on its head. Then it can turn and face its enemies and protect the rest of its body. The "horned dinosaurs" were armoured like this.

A HALF-WAY STAGE

Scientists think that a little dinosaur like this *Psittacosaurus* shows how two-footed plant-eaters (pages 22-25) turned into horned dinosaurs. The square shape of the head is produced by a bony ridge at the neck. This supported the neck and jaw muscles, and later evolved into the neck-shield of the horned dinosaurs. **Which horned dinosaur do you think *Psittacosaurus* could have evolved into?**

Famous armoured plant-eaters

This is how big you would be, compared to the armoured dinosaurs shown on this page.

Try to match up the ages and dates of each of these armoured dinosaurs with the ages and dates of the meat-eaters on pages 16 and 17. Can you see which particular dinosaurs each one had to defend itself against?

Kentrosaurus (pointed lizard). This roofed dinosaur had spines along its back instead of plates. It was 5 metres long and lived in East Africa in the late Jurassic.

Triceratops (three-horned head). This was the biggest and last of the horned dinosaurs. It was 9 metres long and lived in North America at the very end of the Cretaceous.

Stegosaurus (roofed lizard). This is the biggest and best known of the roofed dinosaurs. It had a double row of plates down its back and four spikes on its tail. It was 9 metres long and lived in North America in late Jurassic times.

Protoceratops (first horned head). This was one of the earliest of the horned dinosaurs, not much advanced from *Psittacosaurus* (page 27). It was only about 2 metres long and lived in Mongolia in the early part of the late Cretaceous.

Styracosaurus (spiked lizard). A horned dinosaur which had a single horn on its nose and a neck shield fringed with vicious-looking spikes. It was 6 metres long and lived in North America in the late Cretaceous.

Nodosaurus (knobbly lizard). A welded dinosaur that had its back and sides covered with a tight carpet of small plates. Unlike other welded dinosaurs, it did not have a weapon on its tail. It was 5 metres long and lived in North America in the late Cretaceous.

Euoplocephalus (well-armoured head). And indeed it had! The skull of this welded dinosaur was a rigid box of bone, and it even had armoured eyelids! There was an armour of plates and spines over its back. It had a bony club on its tail to use as a weapon. It was 7 metres long and lived in North America and China in late Cretaceous times.

Flying animals

At the same time as the dinosaurs there lived some flying reptiles called "pterosaurs".

As with most animals, you can tell what pterosaurs ate by looking at their skulls and teeth. **See if you can match up the skulls with the pterosaurs opposite.**

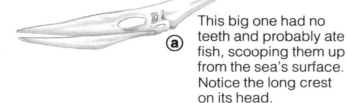

ⓐ This big one had no teeth and probably ate fish, scooping them up from the sea's surface. Notice the long crest on its head.

This pterosaur had two kinds of teeth, and probably ate meat.

ⓑ

ⓒ This skull belonged to one of the smallest pterosaurs. It may have eaten insects.

✦ ANSWERS ✦

Skull ⓐ belongs to *Pteranodon.*

Skull ⓑ was a *Dimorphodon's.*

Pterodactylus was the owner of skull ⓒ.

We can rebuild it!

This is the well-preserved fossil skeleton of a flying animal from the age of the dinosaurs.

When the bones are straightened out, it gives a skeleton like this (a reconstruction).

We can then build up a picture of the animal like this (a restoration).

This flying animal's awkward name, *Rhamphorhynchus*, simply means "narrow beak". After we have found a well-preserved skeleton, it is easy to identify individual bones when we find them separately.

We can tell from the bones of *Rhamphorhynchus* and other pterosaurs, that they were closely related to the dinosaurs. The crocodiles — still around today, of course — are related in the same way.

Make a pterosaur – or two!

Trace the outline shapes printed on pages 38 and 39. Cut the small single pteranodon out of the paper. Use some stiff card to make the wings and body of the larger flyer.

1. Fold the small paper pterosaur along the dotted lines shown on the printed outline.
Staple the body together at the nose end. Make sure that the wings are straight and bent slightly upwards.

2. Gently launch this glider. If it flips down, turn up the feet slightly. If it flips up and then crashes, weight the nose with a piece of sticky tape or two. A little bit of adjustment should get it flying nicely.

3. Fix a wing to each side of the large pterosaur's body with sticky tape.
Make a hole in the centre of each wing, about a third of the way along from the body. Attach a thread or a length of fishing line as shown and hang up the model.

4. To balance the model, put another piece of thread from the nose to the tail and add modelling clay until it makes the wings lie flat. This pterosaur should now flap its wings in a breeze.

Which model do you think behaves most like a real pterosaur did – the glider or the flapper?
Scientists used to think that pterosaurs had a gliding flight. Now the experts have changed their minds and think that these flying reptiles flapped their wings like bats do. They think this because fossil pterosaur fur has been discovered – and it is just like a bat's.

Early bird

Pterosaurs were not birds, but the first birds were around at the same time. This bird is *Archaeopteryx*. It lived at the same time and in the same place as *Rhamphorhynchus* and *Pterodactylus*.

If you took the feathers away, it would look just like one of the small meat-eating dinosaurs – *Compsognathus* shown on page 17. We think that the birds evolved from small meat-eaters like these.

Quetzalcoatlus was named after an ancient Mexican god – a flying snake. It was the biggest pterosaur known, with a wingspan of 12 metres – as big as a light aircraft. It lived in North America in the late Cretaceous.

Pteranodon (winged with no teeth) had a hammer-head with a long crest balancing its toothless jaws. It had a wingspan of 8 metres and lived in North America and Japan in the late Cretaceous.

Dimorphodon (two kinds of teeth). This was one of the earliest pterosaurs – its wingspan was 1.5 metres. It lived in southern England in early Jurassic times.

Pterodactylus (wing finger). This small short-tailed type of flying reptile may have been as small as a sparrow, with a wing span of less than 30 centimetres. It lived in Europe in late Jurassic times.

Swimming reptiles

None of the dinosaurs actually lived in the sea. But many large sea reptiles did exist in the age of the dinosaurs. Here are a few of them.

Elasmosaurus (long reptile). This was one of the longest, reaching 12 metres long. It had over 70 vertebrae in its neck alone! It lived in North America and Japan in late Cretaceous times.

PLESIOSAURS

William Buckland (see page 34) described these as "snakes threaded through the bodies of turtles". That was because their necks were long and thin for darting after prey, but their bodies were round and had paddle-like flippers. They probably "flew" through the water using their paddles like wings.

ICHTHYOSAURS

These were the fish-lizards, shaped just like fish so that they could live comfortably in water. They ate squid-like animals and fish.

PLACODONTS

These looked like big newts. Placodonts had strong crushing teeth for grinding up shellfish. They scraped them from the rocks with their front teeth. Some grew to look like sea turtles.

Ophthalmosaurus (eye lizard). This was one of the largest ichthyosaurs. It had big eyes that helped it to hunt but, unlike its smaller relatives, it had no teeth in its jaws. It was 3 metres long and lived in Europe during the Jurassic period.

Placodus (flat-toothed) was a typical placodont. It was 2 metres long and lived in Europe in middle Triassic times.

Make a plesiosaur

Build a plesiosaur and see how it worked. Make the body from a lump of modelling clay, and stick cardboard paddles on each side. Make a head out of clay and a long neck from a piece of string. Now dangle it in the bath from threads, like a puppet. You will find that the body can move quite slowly, while the head can dart out to catch swift fish.

PLIOSAURS

These were the short-necked plesiosaurs and were big beasts – the whales of the Jurassic and Cretaceous seas. Like the sperm whale of today, they probably ate big squids and squid-like animals.

Kronosaurus (named after a giant in a Greek legend) was a giant of a pliosaur, 17 metres long, from the early Cretaceous of Australia. You would have been able to stand upright in its open jaws!

MOSASAURS

If you can imagine a crocodile living in the sea, with paddles instead of legs, that is what a mosasaur looked like. It was quite closely related to the lizards and snakes. Its triangular jaws were full of sharp strong teeth.

Tylosaurus was one of the biggest mosasaurs. It was 8 metres long, and lived in North America in late Cretaceous times.

Food

Here are some things that lived in the seas in Triassic, Jurassic and Cretaceous times. *Can you work out which animals shown have eaten which of these foods?*

Leptolepis was a Jurassic fish like a herring. It would have swam swiftly away from any slow-moving enemy, unless that creature could suddenly dart after it.

Belemnite A squid-like animal from the Jurassic and Cretaceous periods. It was probably eaten by toothless hunters.

Ammonite This was like a squid with a coiled shell. Fossil shells are sometimes found with tooth marks on them, showing where a strong-jawed animal had chewed them.

Terebratula was one of a group of shellfish called brachiopods. They were common in prehistoric times. Whole banks of them were probably good food for shell-eating animals.

◆*ANSWERS*◆

FOOD

Plesiosaurs would have feasted on *Leptolepis* and other fish. Belemnites and other squid-like animals would have been tasty treats for pliosaurs and ichthyosaurs. Ammonites would have been eaten by pliosaurs, ichthyosaurs and mosasaurs. The shellfish *Terebratula* made a tasty meal for placodonts.

Famous fossil finders

How would you like to be the first person to discover the skeleton of a new fossil reptile? Here are some people who managed to do just this.

MARY ANNING

When she was a little girl living in England on the Dorset coast, Mary Anning helped her father to find fossils to sell in his shop. In 1811, when she was 12 years old, she is supposed to have discovered the first complete ichthyosaur (see page 32), but we now know that this is just a story. The first ichthyosaur was really found by her brother. However, Mary did find the first pterosaur in Britain.

WILLIAM BUCKLAND

One of the first pieces of dinosaur fossil to be discovered was a jaw bone with a meat-eater's tooth still in it. William Buckland named the animal *Megalosaurus* (big lizard) in 1824.

GIDEON MANTELL

A doctor in Sussex, in southern England, Gideon Mantell and his wife Mary, discovered the first *Iguanodon* remains in 1820. He found some of the animal's teeth first (above), but the experts he showed them to didn't know which creature they belonged to.

Eventually Mantell found the rest of the dinosaur's remains in a quarry. He named it *Iguanodon*, as the teeth looked like those of the South American iguana lizard. The fossils were first mentioned publicly in Mantell's book *The Fossils of the South Downs*, which was published in 1822.

EDWARD DRINKER COPE and OTHNIEL CHARLES MARSH

These two were rich men who hated each other. They both organized expeditions to find dinosaur remains in North America's Indian country in the late 1800s. Each man raced to find more fossils than the other one, and their workers often came to blows. Most of the famous dinosaurs that we know today were uncovered by these warring palaeontologists.

Othniel Charles Marsh

Edward Drinker Cope

WILLIAM WALKER

This amateur fossil hunter uncovered an enormous claw in a clay pit in Surrey, England, in 1983. The British Museum (Natural History) excavated the site and found the almost complete skeleton of the meat-eating *Baryonyx* (see page 17). It was as big as a bus, had a head like a crocodile, and had an enormous claw on each hand. It probably lived by scooping fish out of streams, just like grizzly bears do today.

JULES CRETEUR

Jules was a miner, working in a coalmine in Bernissart, Belgium, in 1878. One day, instead of coal, he began to dig out bones. He and his colleagues had stumbled upon a mass of no fewer than 39 complete *Iguanodon* skeletons. This find has provided us with most of our present knowledge about *Iguanodons*.

Very often important finds are made in quarries, where workers accidentally find fossils while cutting out and moving the stone. The biggest ichthyosaur ever found (11 metres long) was uncovered in 1986 in a quarry near Lyon, in France.

Although these people actually made the discoveries, most of the credit for new finds usually goes to the palaeontologist who studies and describes the remains. Quite rightly too, since it is the palaeontologist who makes the collection of dry bones into a "living creature" that we can all appreciate. For example, Jules Creteur's Iguanodons were described by Louis Dollo, and William Walker's Baryonyx is being studied by Alan Charig.

Quiz time

True or False?

Some of these animals are real dinosaurs and really did exist. Others are completely made up. **Which ones do you think are true, and which false?**

1. **Spinosaurus**. A flesh-eating dinosaur from the early Cretaceous of West Africa. It has a big fin on its back, possibly to help it to keep cool.

2. **Chasmosaurus**. A horned plant-eater with an enormous frill. It lived in the late Cretaceous of North America.

3. **Pachycephalosaurus.** A two-footed plant-eater from the late Cretaceous of North America. It had a thick dome of bone on its head and may have used this against enemies as a battering ram.

4. **Aeolosaurus.** One of the welded dinosaurs, with a large, heavy body. Scientists have found skin impressions which show that it had gliding wings stretched between its legs. It lived in North Africa in late Jurassic times.

5. **Rhedosaurus**. A four-footed flesh-eater from the late Cretaceous of North America. It lived on other dinosaurs which it caught using its sharp teeth and claws.

Open Wide

These teeth are from animals you have seen in this book. **Which ones do they belong to?**

1. This is the roof of the mouth of a fossil reptile. The peg-like teeth at the front were for picking something off a rock, and the broad flat teeth on the palate must have been for crushing something very hard.

2. Here you can see dozens of rough teeth compacted together in a jaw, like dates in a date box. They must have been used for grinding down something tough, like pine-needles.

3. These leaf-like teeth belonged to a plant-eater as well. See how some of them have been worn down by chewing. The scientists who first found them thought that they looked like the teeth of the modern iguana lizard.

Who went there?

If you saw these footprints in a rock, what kind of dinosaur would you say made them?

1. These footprints were the size of tea-trays and were made by one of the longest four-footed plant-eating dinosaurs.

2. These are from a two-footed animal. The footprints look a bit like birds' footprints. What do you think made that scrape up the middle?

3. These are from another two-footed animal. They have big claws on the toes.

Index

Glossary

Amphibian An animal which lives as a tadpole in the water when young, but spends its adult life on land. Frogs and newts are amphibians.

Bed A single layer of *sedimentary rock*.

Conifer A cone-bearing tree. Conifers are usually evergreen, with needles instead of leaves.

Era A large division of geological time, usually lasting tens of millions of years. Each era consists of a number of *periods*.

Fossil The remains of a plant or animal found preserved in rock. Fossils are usually made of the hard parts of the animal or plant. The original material is often turned into stone. Footprints preserved in the rock are also fossils.

Horse-tail A primitive plant like a fern, with rings of narrow leaves growing from the joints of its stem.

Mammal An animal that gives birth to live babies and then looks after them. Mammals are usually hairy. Most of today's animals – including humans – are mammals.

Period A division of geological time. Different animals lived during different periods. Experts can tell the periods apart by studying the different fossils that were formed during them.

Pterosaur A flying reptile from the Mesozoic era. There were many types of pterosaur, but each had a furry body and leathery wings.

Reconstruction The bones of a fossil animal, put together to form a skeleton.

Reptile An animal that has a scaly skin and hatches from an egg on land. Lizards, snakes and crocodiles are reptiles. So were dinosaurs.

Restoration A picture or a model made to show what a fossil animal would have looked like when it was alive.

Sedimentary rock Rock made of layers of loose material, like sand or mud. The sand or mud was turned into rock by being buried and cemented together by minerals.

Skull The structure of bones inside an animal's head, including the bones that make the brain-box, the face and the jaws.

Vertebra One of the bones of the backbone, whether from the neck, the body or the tail. More than one vertebra are called vertebrae.

Vertebrate Any animal with a backbone. Fish, amphibians, reptiles, birds and mammals are all vertebrates.